D0195135

WILD WISDOM

For Didy and Robby,

and to the

memory of Scott.

Furry Logic

WILD WISDOM

Jane Seabrook

10
TEN SPEED PRESS
Berkeley | Toronto

Life can be very deep,

but I'm trying to stay at the

shallow end.

I'd rather

have **too much** *too soon*

than too little too late.

Happy people are more

likely to get what they want —

which only makes them

even more happy.

I want what I want

when I want it!

Apart from that, I'm

quite easy to please.

The greatest wealth is to be rich in friends —

but if possible let them be

rich friends.

Of course we're friends –

you know I'd share my last

piece of trouble with you.

For your own safety,

please stay behind the line

I have drawn around

my supply of chocolate.

Gossip is when you

hear something you like

about someone you don't.

The facts may be against me,

but all the *illusions*

are on my side.

Anybody who tries to get

between me and my work

has a good chance of succeeding.

Wake me up

when everything is organized.

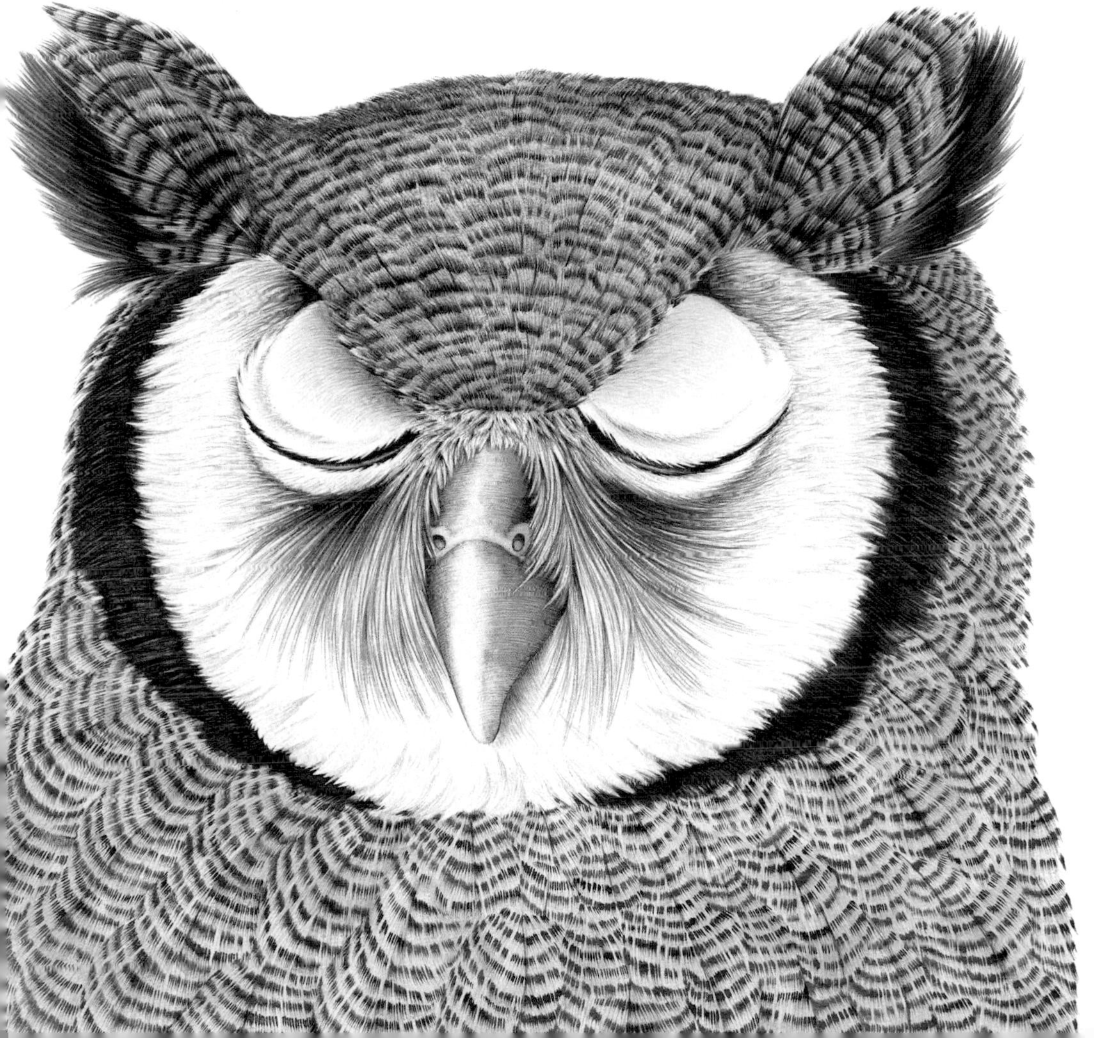

By doing just a little every day,

I can gradually let the task

completely overwhelm me.

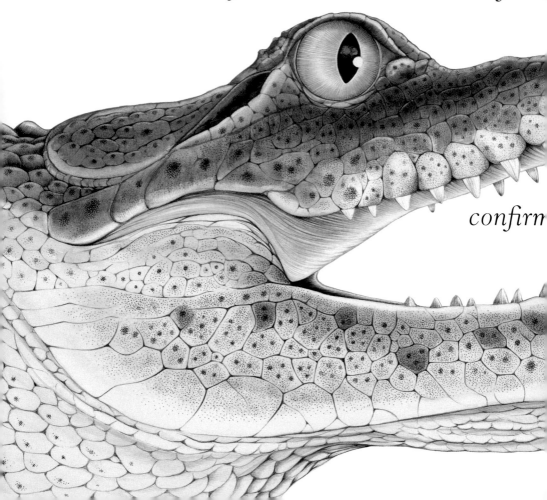

I'd like to show you who's boss but am afraid

confirm

t would only

hat you are.

Please don't tell me to relax —

it's only

ny tension that's holding me together.

Another day, another dither.

If men weren't

so simple,

women

wouldn't

have to be so

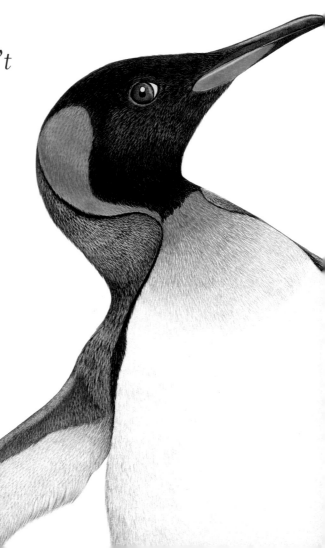

complicated.

You have

the ability

to arouse

various

emotions

in me:

please

select

carefully.

And please keep your mind open

until I can get a little more of my

argument into it.

Is it

you and I

who are crazy,

or is it

everybody

else?

Don't worry—

I'll stay with you all the way to the

end of your

money.

You brought something

into my life I never

had before:

your mother.

Please don't try to

change my bad habits—

they're all I've got!

I'm looking for a party

where I can be the designated

eater.

Inside every older person

there's a younger person

wondering what happened.

I'm hoping to take another bite

out of life before life

takes another

bite out of me.

There has been an alarming

increase in the number of things

I know nothing about.

My life is very

delicately balanced.

Please don't make any

sudden   movements.

If the meaning of life

doesn't soon become clear,

I may have to

request an extension.

Christmas is coming,

and I don't know how to get out

of its way.

Your order for lessons in patience

has been received — please allow

four to six months for delivery.

Artist's Notes

When painting for *Furry Logic,* it is always fun discovering an animal or bird that I have never heard of before — especially a crazy-looking bird like this aracari. In case you ever get a trivia question on aracaris, they are a member of the toucan family but smaller and with a more slender bill. At the other end of the scale, the toco toucan is the largest member of the toucan family and purely by coincidence these birds are on consecutive pages in the book.

I hope you have enjoyed this new collection of *Furry Logic,* and I always look forward to receiving your comments and suggestions via my website.

Best wishes, Jane.

For more information,
including how to purchase any of
the original paintings that appear
in this book, visit www.furrylogicbooks.com.

Furry Logic Who's Who

Because I'm sometimes asked to identify the animals and birds I've painted, I've named them here — from the familiar and recognizable to the more unusual among them such as the magnificent cock-of-the-rock, the strawberry poison-dart frog and the strange-looking aracari. In order of appearance they are:

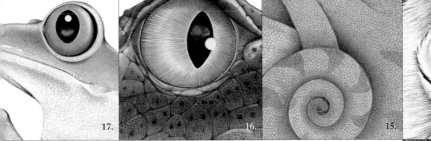

1. Rockhopper penguin 2. Chipmunk 3. Giant panda

4. Siberian tiger 5. Golden pheasant 6. Cock-of-the-rock

7. Peacock 8. Green tree frog 9. Mandrill 10. Impala

11. Yellow-billed oxpecker 12. Major Mitchell's cockatoo

13. Grizzly bear 14. Eagle owl 15. Chameleon

16. American crocodile 17. Green tree frog

18. Strawberry poison-dart frog 19. Chipmunk

20. King penguin

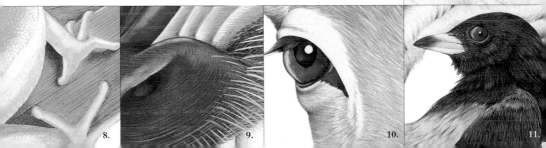

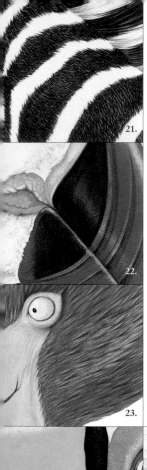

Furry Logic Who's Who

21. Boehm's zebra 22. Atlantic puffin 23. Lesser flamingo
24. Toco toucan 25. Aracari 26. Fruit bat 27. Pig
28. Lemur 29. Grevy's zebra 30. Meerkat 31. Ladybug
32. Red-eyed tree frog 33. Red cardinal 34. Grizzly bear

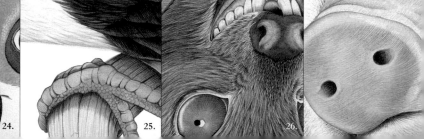

Other Books by Jane Seabrook

Furry Logic: A Guide to Life's Little Challenges

Furry Logic Parenthood

Furry Logic Laugh at Life

The Pick of Furry Logic

For more information visit www.furrylogicbooks.com.

34.

33.

32.

28.

29.

30.

31.

Thank you!

Acknowledgments

Grateful thanks to Ashleigh Brilliant for permission to reproduce the quotations that appear in this book. With the exception of "Gossip is when you hear something you like about someone you don't" (Earl Wilson), all quotes are from the Ashleigh Brilliant Pot-Shot series. "And please keep your mind open until I can get a little more of my argument into it" is derived from the original Pot-Shot #3195, "Please keep your mind open until I can get a little more of my argument into it"; copyright ©1977 by Ashleigh Brilliant.

For thousands more Ashleigh Brilliant Pot-Shots or for more information about his work, visit www.ashleighbrilliant.com.

Thank you to everyone at Ten Speed Press for all their support and encouragement, especially Lorena Jones, Meghan Keeffe, and Kristine Standley.

Thank you also to Alex Trimbach and Troy Caltaux at Image Centre in Auckland, New Zealand, and to Debby Heard Photography, Joy Willis, and Phoenix Offset.

Ten Speed Press
P O Box 7123, Berkeley, California 94707, United States
www.tenspeed.com

Distributed in Canada by Ten Speed Press Canada.

Library of Congress Cataloging-in-Publication Data
is on file with the publisher.

ISBN-13: 978-1-58008-816-9
ISBN-10: 1-58008-816-3

Printed in China
First printing, 2007

1 2 3 4 5 6 7 8 9 10 — 11 10 09 08 07